My African Kitchen Cookbook

GBELEE SUMO

To order additional copies of this book, contact:
Xlibris
1-888-795-4274
www.Xlibris.com
Orders@Xlibris.com

About Cook Book

African meals are generally very rich in nutrients, fibers and antioxidants. African cooking is about throwing all the ingredients together while relishing the aroma and tasting the flavours as you cook. "My African Kitchen" cook book gives a choice to the amateurs as well as professional cooks to add and subtract ingredients and still have healthy and delicious meals. The cooking methods employed in "My African Kitchen cook book" involve the use of minimal fat while retaining the natural flavors of the food, as the meals are often steamed, boiled, or baked. The book also includes few recipes which are fried, to give them an appetising flavour. My African Kitchen cook book contains traditional and healthy recipes based on the whole and unprocessed ingredients. These meals are full of variety of nutritious ingredients. This book includes traditional African recipes that have been passed on from one generation to another. My African Kitchen cook book has a collection of recipes that deliver the flavours of Africa. Each recipe in this book is presented in easy to follow steps which cater for broad audience appealing for beginners to advanced level cooks.

Note: All stoves and ovens are not of the same quality. Therefore, use appropriate and suggested temperature while cooking. Please keep that in mind while preparing all the recipes in this cook book.

Slow Baked Lamb Meat

Ingredients

- 3lb and 4.9oz of Lamb
- 1 and 1/2 of Knorr
- 1 and 1/2 of garlic powder
- 1 tbsp. of white pepper powder
- 1/2 of pink salt

Instructions

- Cut the lamb into the piece you want and put them in a large bowl
- Add the Knorr, garlic, black pepper and salt to the lamb
- Mix or toss the lamb to properly season
- After mixing the seasoning, keep refrigerated
- When ready to bake, lay out the meat pieces individually on a large baking tray
- Slow bake the lamb for an hour and serve hot

Note

For a well-seasoned meat, leave the seasoning over night or first thing in the morning before baking for dinner

Fried Okra Strew

Ingredients

- 840 kg or okra
- One medium onion
- A bunch of green onions
- 1/2 and 1/3 cup of palm oil
- 1 tbsp. and 1/2 of Knorr
- 1/2 of pink salt
- Meat (fried and any amount)
- 8 cups of water
- Hot peppers (optional)

Instructions

- Wash and thinly slice the okra and put the sliced okra into a separate bowl
- Keep the sliced okra on the side and get a large pot
- Slice a medium onion and the green onions
- Put the oil into a pot, put the pot on the stove on high heat and let the oil warm up
- When the oil is warm, add the sliced onions and fry on a medium flame until the onions turn brown
- When brown, add the sliced okra and stir-fry until its slime free (fry for 30 minutes)
- To prevent the okra from burning; keep adjusting the stove as you stir-fry
- When okra is slime free and well fried; add water, Knorr, meat and salt
- Stir and cook the okra on high heat for 30 minutes
- When the water starts to dry off, lower the stove and frequently check and stir as it cooks
- Pertinently cook and stir the okra on low or medium heat until the water dries off
- When you start to see more oil than water, it means ready
- When the sauce is cooked nicely then add salt (if needed, and enjoy your meal)

Notes

Palm oil is used to prepare this recipe but it is optional. You can prepare this recipe with olive or any oil of your choice. Follow the same measurement in the ingredients section. When the seeds of the okra are white, it means it is not cooked. When the okra is slime free and the seeds are brown, it means it is well cooked.

Fried Eggplants Stew

Ingredients

- 8 baby eggplants
- 2 large Mackerel fish (fried)
- 1/2 and 1/3 cup of olive oil
- 4 medium fresh tomatoes (chopped)

- 1 large onion (sliced)
- A bunch of green onions (sliced)
- 6 cups of water
- 3 tbsp. of Knorr
- 1/2 tsp of salt
- Hot peppers (optional)

Instructions

- First, clean and cut the fish into the pieces as per your choice
- Wash the fish with lemon juice and rinse well to properly wash off the lemon
- Season the fish then put it into a large bowl and cover with a lid, keep refrigerated
- Peel and thinly slice the eggplants into a large bowl and keep it aside
- Slice and chop the fresh ingredients and keep them on the side as well
- Fry the fish in a frying pan or a deep-fryer until they are golden brown or crispy
- Keep the fried fish on the side and start preparing the eggplants
- Get a large pot, put the oil into it, keep the pot on the stove and set on high heat
- Warm the oil and add the fresh sliced and chopped ingredients

- Stir fry the fresh ingredients until soften and then add the sliced eggplants
- Without adding water yet, stir and fry the eggplants for 15 minutes
- Do not leave the eggplants unattended or it might burn
- After nearly15 minutes, add the water, Knorr, salt, stir and let it cook
- As the eggplant cooks, check frequently and stir
- When water starts to dry off, add the fish carefully and stir
- If the sauce starts to burn at the bottom, set the stove on medium heat
- Cook and carefully stir frequently until the water dries off completely
- When you get a satisfactory texture then taste it and add salt if needed

Notes

It takes a lot of patience to completely dry off the eggplant stew. It requires frequent stirring. When the oil starts to settle on the stew, it means it is about ready

Fried Chicken Wings

Ingredients

- 8lbs of chicken wings
- 1 tsp of Knorr
- 1/2 tsp of garlic powder
- 1/2 tsp of black pepper
- 1/2 tsp of onion powder
- 1/2 of white pepper powder
- 1/8 tsp of pink salt

Instructions

- Put the chicken into a large bowl that has a lid to it
- Add all the ingredients and toss well
- After tossing the chicken, put the lid and keep refrigerated (this can be done overnight or first thing in the morning)
- When ready, fry the chicken to your satisfaction (you can use the deep-fryer or frying pan)

Notes

This recipe can also be made into a party size portions. If you decide to make 16lbs, all you need to do is double the ingredients and measurement.

Smoked fish Kale dish

Ingredients

- 3 bunch of Kale
- A cup and 1/3 of Olive oil
- 1 large onion (slice)
- A bunch of green onions (slice)
- 1 tsp of baking soda
- 3 cups of water
- Knorr 2 tbsp. and ½
- Pink salt ½ tsp
- Smoked fish (any amount)
- Hot peppers (optional)

Instructions

- Wash the kale with cold water and chop it into small pieces and wash it again with cold water then use a large strainer to drain
- Put the washed kale into a large pot and add 4/ ½ cup of cold water; let the kale steam for 3 to 4 minutes
- After steaming wash again and drain in a large strainer; if you don't like your kale steamed, skip and go to the next step
- Put the drained kale into a large bowl, put a lid and keep on the side for the main time
- Get a large pot, put the oil into the pot and add the sliced onions; set the stove on high. Mix and fry the onions for 3 minutes; after 3 minutes, add the kale to the fried onions in the pot
- Add a tsp of baking soda and stir well for at least one minute (the baking soda will give the kale a greenish color)
- After a minute, add water, fish, Knorr and salt; cook the kale until water is completely dried off
- When water starts to dry off, set the stove on medium heat or low to prevent the kale from burning
- Check and stir frequently until water dries off completely
- When dry to your satisfaction, add Knorr or salt, if needed and enjoy your meal.

Notes

The three bunch of kale prepared in this recipe was bought from the green house. The bunch of kale from the grocery store might not be the same as the one from the green house. Please keep that in mind while making this dish. Eating the kale with steam rice is optional. You can serve the kale with whatever you want.

Meatballs Stew

Meatballs ingredients

- Ground beef = 750 gram
- Half medium onion
- 2 ¼ times 2 cup of milk
- 2 slices of bread
- 1 Tsp of Knorr
- 1/4 Tsp of pink salt
- 1 Tsp of black pepper
- Stew Ingredients
- 4 medium tomatoes
- 2 medium onions
- A bunch of green onions
- 1 tsp of black pepper
- ½ cup of olive oil
- 1 Tsp of Knorr
- 1/4 Tsp of pink salt
- 1 cup of water

Stew Ingredients

- 4 medium tomatoes
- 2 medium onions
- A bunch of green onions
- 1 tsp of black pepper
- ½ cup of olive oil
- 1 Tsp of Knorr
- 1/4 Tsp of pink salt
- 1 cup of water
- Hot peppers (optional)

Meatballs Instructions

- Put the ground meat into a large bowl and add the Knorr, salt and black pepper and mix properly.
- Put the half onion into a blender, add the milk and blend
- Put the blended onions into a bowl, add two slice of bread and scramble
- Add the scrambled bread to the ground meat and mix properly
- When properly mixed, make the meat into balls and place them on a baking tray
- Set the oven to 350 degree, preheat and bake the meat balls for 25 minutes
- After baking, put the oil into a frying pan and fry the meat balls until they are brown.
- When the meat balls are nice and fried, put them into a bowl, put the lid and keep on the side while you are getting the stew ready

Stew instructions

- Clean all the wet ingredients and put them into a food processor and chop (if you don't have a food processor, thinly slice the wet ingredients)
- Put the wet ingredients into a large pot and add the black pepper, oil, Knorr and salt
- Put the pot on the stove on medium heat and cook until soften
- Add the water and set the stove on high; when the stew starts to thicken, add the meat balls and stir carefully
- Set the stove on medium heat and cook the stew until you are satisfied

Salt Fish Stew

Ingredients

- 4 medium tomatoes
- 2 large onions
- A bunch of parsley
- A bunch of green onions
- 6 fresh garlic
- ½ cup of oil
- 3 cups of water
- 1 and ½ tsp of Knorr chickenbroth
- ½ tsp of salt
- Hot peppers (optional)

Fish prepping

- Cut the salt fish into pieces
- Put the fish into a large pot that has a lid
- Add enough cold water to cover the entire fish
- Keep the fish refrigerated
- Change the water on the fish three times a day for two days
- When the fish is salt free, fry the fish until they turn golden brown or crispy

Stew Instructions

- Put the oil into a large pot
- Wash and chop the tomatoes, onions, parsley, garlic and green onions in a food processor
- Add the chopped ingredients to the oil in the pot
- Put the pot on the stove on high heat
- Cook and stir at the same time until soften (it should take 5 minutes to soften)
- When soften, add the water, Knorr chicken broth and salt
- Stir and add the fish with care; put the lid on the pot and let the stew cook until it starts to thicken
- When it starts to thicken, stir the stew carefully and set the stove on medium heat
- As the stew cooks on medium heat check frequently and stir careful to prevent the fish from falling apart

- Keep cooking and checking on the stew until you are satisfied with the texture
- When get the satisfactory texture then taste and add more salt or Knorr if needed

Notes

This recipe is great for the weekend. You can prep the fish during the week and make a delicious meal during the weekend. Once the salt fish is salt free, the recipe is fast and easy to prepare.

Peanut Soup

Ingredients

- Fresh dill leaf (thinly chopped)
- 1 medium onion
- A bunch of green onions
- 2 medium tomatoes
- 5 garlic
- 1 tbsp. of tomato paste
- 4 ½ cup of water
- 3 tbsp. of smooth peanut butter
- 2 tbsp. of Knorr
- 3 bay leaves
- ½ tsp of salt
- Hot peppers (optional)

Instructions

- Clean, cut and season the fish with Knorr, salt, garlic powder, black pepper and fry until golden brown
- Thinly chop the dill, onion, green onions, tomatoes, garlic and put them into a large pot
- Without adding water, set the stove on high heat, stir and cook until soften (at least for five minutes)
- When soften, add the tomato paste, water, Knorr, salt bay leaves and three big scoops of smooth peanut butter
- Cook the soup on high heat for twenty minutes
- After twenty minutes, carefully add the fried fish and stir with care
- Let the soup cook until it starts to thicken; when it starts to thicken, set the stove on medium heat
- When the soup thickens to your satisfaction, carefully stir and add more salt or Knorr, if needed

Notes

The peanut soup can be served with whatever you want. When the soup is finished and you want to taste it, do not use your finger. Always use a separate and clean spoon to taste or serve the soup. Peanut soup needs T.L.C.

Collard Green

Ingredients

- 1 big bunch of collard greens
- 1 bunch of green onions
- 1 large onion
- 4 cups of extra virgin olive oil
- 1 tbsp. of Knorr
- 4 cups of water
- Fry chicken (any amount)
- Hot peppers (optional)

Instructions

- Wash and thinly slice the greens
- After slicing the greens, wash again and use a large strainer to drain
- While the greens are draining, thinly slice the onion and green onions
- Put a cup of oil into a large pot, set the stove on high heat, warm the oil and add the sliced onions to the oil
- Brown the onions and then add the collard greens
- Stir and fry the greens for five to six minutes
- After five minutes or so, add the water, Knorr, salt and the fried chicken
- Stir, put the lid on the pot and let the greens cook until the water starts to dry off
- When the water starts to dry off, set the stove on medium or low heat to prevent the greens from burning at the bottom
- Frequently check and stir the greens until the water is completely dried off
- When the greens are nice and dry, taste and add more salt of Knorr, if needed

Notes

Please remember that the bunch of collard greens may vary. The bunch of collard greens in this recipe came straight from the green house.

Fried Sweet Potatoes

Ingredients

- 2 sweet potatoes (1 lb 3.8oz and 1 lb. 4.4oz)
- 4 cups of water
- 1 tbsp. of salt (more or less)
- Oil for the frying pan or deep-fryer

Instructions

- Peel two big sweet potatoes and thinly slice
- After slicing, put four cups of water into a large bowl
- Add one tablespoon of salt to the water (if you like extra salt, add another tablespoon)
- Whisk until the salt dissolves and add the sliced sweet potatoes
- Mix the potatoes with your hands and leave the potatoes in the salted water for five minutes
- After five minutes, drain the potatoes in a large strainer
- When the potatoes are drained, fry until they turn golden brown (you can use the deep-fryer or frying pan)

Notes

This recipe is great for game nights, snacks or a get together. You can make your own dipping sauce to serve with the fried potatoes.

Green Lentil Dish

Ingredients

- 2 cups of Green Lentils
- 12/ ½ cups of water
- 1 tsp of Pink salt
- 2 tbsp. of Knorr
- 1 large onion (thinly sliced)
- 2 medium tomatoes
- A bunch of green onions
- 1 tbsp. of tomato paste
- ½ cup of oil
- Fried chicken or meat (any amount)
- Hot peppers (optional)

Instructions

- Wash and put the green lentils into a large pot
- Add the water, salt, Knorr and cook on high heat until the lentils are soft
- While beans are cooking, prepare the chicken or meat you want to cook with lentils
- When lentils are well cooked, put the cooked lentils into a bowl
- Wash the pot that you cooked the lentils in and get ready to finish the last step
- Slice one large onion, 2 medium tomatoes and a bunch of green onions
- Put the pot on the stove, set on high heat and add ½ cup of oil
- Warm up the oil and add all the sliced ingredients
- Without adding water, stir and cook until soften
- When soften, add a tablespoon of tomato paste and the chicken or meat
- Stir well, add the cooked lentils, add a cup of water and mix or stir properly
- Cook for five minutes and after five minutes set the stove on medium heat
- Check and stir frequently until you are satisfied with the texture
- When satisfied, taste and add salt or Knorr if needed

Cassava Leaf dish

Ingredients

- Cassava leaf - 2.2lb
- 4 medium eggplants
- 1 large onion
- A bunch of green onions
- 14 cups of water
- 1 tsp of pink salt
- 3 tbsp. of Knorr
- 2 large tilapia fish
- 2 cups of palm oil
- Hot peppers (optional)

Instructions

- Put the cassava leaf into an extra-large pot; peel and chop the eggplants, onion and green onions
- Blend and add to the cassava leaf (if you do not have a blender, use the food processor)
- After adding the blended ingredients to the cassava leaf, add the water, salt and Knorr
- Cover the pot and cook on high heat for about two hours (cooking time may vary depending on the stove type)
- While the cassava leaf is cooking, start to prepare the fish; clean, wash the fish with lemon juice and rinse properly
- Put the fish in a large pot, add enough water to cover the entire fish and boil on high heat for 30 to 40 minutes
- Put the boiled fish in a bowl; carefully add the fish broth to the cassava leaf
- When the water starts to dry off, set the stove on medium heat, check and stir frequently
- While the cassava leaf is cooking on medium heat, carefully take the fish off the bones and add the bone free fish to the cassava leaf
- After adding the fish, stir to properly mix the fish with the cassava leaf; now it is time get the oil ready
- Put two cups of palm oil into a small pot and heat up on high heat for about three minute
- Carefully add the heated oil to the cassava leaf (be very careful with your eyes. If you have to wear safety goggles, please do so)

- After adding the oil, stir and cook the cassava leaf until the water dry off (frequently stir adjust the stove)
- Taste and add salt or Knorr if needed (when you are satisfied with the texture, enjoy your meal)

Note

To make this recipe, you are going to need an extra-large pot. This dish is not a quick 30 minutes' meal. It is great to prepare this dish on the weekend or during your days off from work. Tilapia fish is optional. You can make this recipe with boneless fish, shrimp, meat or chicken.

Fried Plantains

Instructions

- Peel the plantains by making one incision inside the plantain skin
- Slice them diagonally (not too thick and not too thin)
- Put the sliced plantains into a large bowl, sprinkle salt and toss
- Heat frying pan with enough oil to cover the slices (you can also use the deep-fryer if you want)
- Fry plantain slices until golden brown on each side
- Each side needs about a minute to cook (be careful not to burn)
- Place fried plantains in a plate layered with napkin to drain the oil
- Serve the dish as you choose

Water Greens Torborgee

Ingredients

- 2 bunch of water greens/ spinach
- 1 medium onion
- A bunch of green onions
- 8 cups of water
- 1 tbsp. of Knorr
- 1/2 tsp of pink salt
- Meat (any amount and sear)
- 1/2 cup of Palm oil
- Hot peppers (optional)
- 1 tsp of baking soda (more or less)

Instructions

- Wash the fresh water greens with cold water
- Thinly slice the water greens, parboil and wash again
- Put the washed greens into a large pot
- Slice both onions and add them to the greens
- Add the water, Knorr, salt and meat
- Cook on high heat until the water starts to dry
- Add the palm and let greens cook until the greens start to thicken
- When sauce is thick to your satisfaction, taste and add salt, if needed
- Turn off or set the stove on low heat
- Add the baking or country soda bit by bit and stir at the same time
- Enjoy your Torborgee with steamed rice

Note

This recipe can be prepared with fish, chicken, shrimps, lobsters and so on. Just make sure the fish is fried and sear the meat, chicken, shrimp.

Spinach and fish

Fish Ingredients

- 6 golden bisugo fish
- 1 tsp of Onion powder
- 1 tsp of garlic powder
- A pinch of salt
- ½ tsp of Knorr

Spinach Ingredients

- 4 bunch of spinach
- 4 cup of water (32 OZ)
- One sliced onion
- One tsp of Pink salt
- One tsp. of Knorr
- One bunch of green onion
- Extra virgin olive oil (1 cup)
- Hot pepper (Optional)

Preparing the spinach

- Wash and thinly slice 4 bunch of fresh spinach
- After slicing the spinach, put it in a large pot, steam, wash and strain
- After straining the steamed spinach, put it in a large cooking pot
- Add the water and all the wet and dry ingredients including the oil
- Cook until the water dries off completely
- When the spinach is nice and dry, get ready to prepare the fish

Preparing the fish

- Put the fish in a large bowl that has lid
- Add all the spices and seasoning to the fish
- Toss the fish for proper seasoning (overnight or first thing in the morning)
- When you are ready to prepare the fish fry to your satisfaction

Notes

This dish is fast and easy to make for your family. Season the fish over night or first thing in the morning. You can fry the fish in the deep-fryer or you can use a frying pan.

Fried Tilapia Fish

Ingredients

- One yellow bell pepper
- Half onion and half fresh tomato
- ½ tsp of Knorr
- ¼ tsp of pink salt
- 3 fresh garlic
- Two tbsp. of olive oil
- Hot peppers (optional)

Instructions

- Put all the ingredients in a blender or a food processor
- After blending or processing all the ingredients put the fish in a large bowl that has a lid
- Add the blended ingredients to the fish and mix well
- Keep the fish in the fridge over night or do the process first thing in the morning and keep the fish in the fridge
- When ready, fry the fish in a deep fryer or use a frying pan and fry the fish to your satisfaction

Lamb Stew

Ingredients

- Lamb chops (0.948 kg)
- Water (4 cup and a half)
- 3 sliced medium tomatoes
- One Onion (thinly sliced)
- Pink salt (one tsp)
- One tbsp. of Knorr
- 6 garlic (thinly sliced)
- 4 Bay leaves
- Hot peppers (optional)

Instructions

- Wash the lamb meat, put them into a bowl and keep it aside
- Put all the fresh ingredients into a large pot
- Without adding oil cook on medium heat until soften
- When soften, add the lamb, water and the rest of the ingredients
- Cook the stew until it thickens
- When you are satisfied with the texture of the stew, taste and add salt, if needed

Notes

This stew can be made for small or large family and it can be eaten with any side dish of your choice.

Joll of Rice

Rice Ingredients

- 4 medium size skinless tomatoes
- One large onion
- 5 Garlic
- Knorr chicken broth mixed 2 tbsp.
- Pink Salt ½ tsp
- Black pepper 1 tsp
- Tomato paste 2 tbsp.
- 4 cups of water
- 2 cups of long grain rice
- 5 tbsp. of oil (more or less)
- Fried chicken or Smoked sausages
- Hot peppers (optional)

Rice Preparation

- Put 4 cups of water into a large pot
- Put the tomatoes, onion and garlic into a food processor and chop
- Put the chopped ingredients into the pot including the Knorr, salt, black pepper and tomato paste
- Set the stove on high heat and cook for 15 minutes
- After 15 minutes, rinse and add two cups of long grain rice
- Stir and cook uncovered until tender but still slightly chewy
- When it starts to become crusty at the bottom, turn the stove off
- Cover and let the rice rest for ten minutes, add the oil and stir
- Cover, simmer for twenty minutes and then bring back to a gentle simmer
- Reduce heat to low and cook until the water is absorbed
- When the rice is nice and fluffy, it is ready to serve
- Peel, slice and fry the plantains as a side dish or a fried fish

Notes

If you don't like plantains, you can use any side dish of your choice with rice.

Oven Boiled Pangasius Fish

Ingredients

- 1.459 Lb of fish
- 2 bunch of green onion (slice)
- 3 sliced medium fresh tomatoes
- 2 sliced onion
- 5 sliced fresh garlic
- tsp of Pink Himalayan Salt
- tsp of Knorr Chicken broth mix
- Fresh hot pepper (optional)

Instructions

- Defrost, wash and season the fish with the dry ingredients (overnight or for three hours)
- When ready to oven boil, spread out a large heavy duty aluminum foil paper in a deep baking pan
- First, put the seasoned fish in the middle of the foil paper and then add all of the fresh ingredients
- Wrap up the fish in the foil paper and leave it in the same spot in the baking pan
- Preheat the oven and set it on high heat and put the fish in the oven and let it boil for an hour

Notes

When preparing this dish, it will be easier to buy the Pangasius fist chunks. To prepare this dish, you are going to need a heavy-duty aluminum foil paper.

Tilapia Fish Soup

Ingredients

- 2 Tilapia fish
- 2 medium onion (thinly sliced)
- 3 medium tomatoes (thinly sliced)
- Green onions leaves (thinly sliced)
- 6 fresh garlic (thinly sliced)
- A tbsp. of Knorr (chicken broth)
- A tsp of pink salt
- Hot peppers (optional)
- 4 cups of water

Instructions

- Clean and cut the fish into two piece
- Put the fish into a large bowl and wash the fish with lemon juice and rinse properly with cold water
- Put the fish into a large pot and add all of the ingredients including water
- Cook the soup until you are satisfied with the texture of the soup
- Taste and add additional salt or Knorr, if needed

Notes

This soup can be made with any kind of fish. When preparing this dish, follow your taste and you can add your favorite vegetables too.

VEGETABLE RICE

Ingredients

- 5 cups of water
- 2 cups of long grain rice
- 1 tbsp. of garlic powder
- 1 tsp of white pepper powder
- 1 tbsp. of curry powder
- 2 tbsp. of Knorr
- 1 tsp of pink salt
- 4 tbsp of olive oil
- 4 cups of vegetables

Instructions

- Rinse the rice and keep on the side
- Put water in a large that has a lid
- Add the white pepper, curry, Knorr, salt and the oil to the water
- Boil uncovered water on high heat for three minutes
- Add the rice, stir and cook uncovered until tender but still slightly chewy
- When it starts to become crusty at the bottom, turn the stove off
- Cover and let the rice rest for ten minutes
- After five minutes, add the vegetables and stir
- Cover, simmer for twenty minutes and then bring back to a gentle simmer
- Reduce heat to low and cook until the water is absorbed
- When the rice is nice and fluffy, it is ready to serve

Printed in the United States
By Bookmasters